The Battle of Lewes 1264

by
E.L. MANN

S.B. Publications

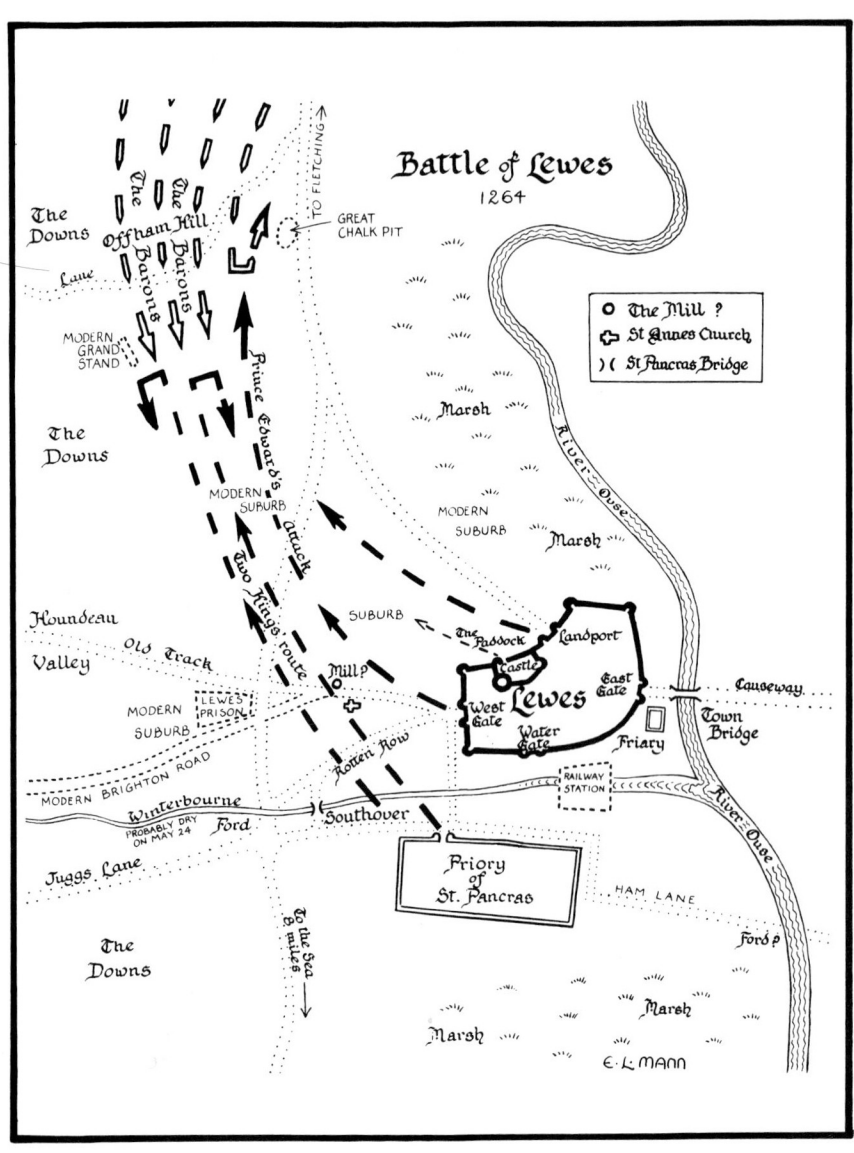

CONTENTS

Foreword	3
Significance	4
The Armies	4
Why at Lewes	5
The Participants	6
Arms and Armour	11
The Action	15
Notes	27

FOREWORD

There is a small field lying on the edge of the wide flat lands to the south of the County Town of Lewes. Underfoot, the ground is humped and broken and from the weeds on every side rise the ruined walls of an ancient monastery whose relics are so vast even now that it is plain that one stands on the site of one of the large religious establishments of mediaeval times.

The church itself stood across the track of the present railway. It was as big as Chichester Cathedral, and nothing of it remains above ground, whatever may still lie beneath the nurseryman's plants. Around it were the monastic buildings whose desecrated remnants we see: the cloisters, the dormitories, the guest house, the two refectories, the almonry, the kitchen, the dovecot and offices of the great Priory of St. Pancras, Lewes.

It is here, actually in the Chapter House, that the Mise of Lewes, celebrated as a foundation of Parliamentary Government was made by Simon de Montfort and Henry III. Seven hundred years later the unique memorial was set up by a generous Member of Parliament representing Lewes at Westminster.

SIGNIFICANCE

The Battle of Lewes is given some importance in our history books because historians trace democratic government back to the agreement signed by the defeated king at the end of the day's fighting.

Seven hundred years ago the people of England were engaged in the Barons' War. It was a civil war. King Henry III and his friends on the one side opposed Simon de Montfort and his followers on the other.

Simon has been regarded as the hero of democracy and Henry as the champion of tyranny. But the issues with which they were concerned were too complicated for that, being a medley of economic, religious, feudal, political and personal interests. It is sufficient here to say that the King's objects and methods of government did not accord with the requirements of some of the wealthier subjects: that some of these assembled under the leadership of Simon and set out to obtain possession of the King in person, to separate him from "bad company": and that enough of the nobility adhered to the King to enable him to make a stand against coercion by Simon.

THE ARMIES

The national armies of later times bear no comparison with those of the Middle Ages. The word "army" to us means a highly trained mass of paid, disciplined troops, obedient and "faithful unto death", conditioned by months or years of co-ordinated activity, organised to carry out all the manoeuvres of their period, working indeed like a machine controlled by one qualified commander. This is generally known as a standing army. The components are all paid professional soldiers.

Nothing like such a force existed at the time of the Battle of Lewes.

Those who recall the Home Guard (not *"Dad's Army"*) of the Second World War will have a fair idea of what the feudal armies of de Montfort's day were like: spare time soldiers. Though many of the Home Guard had seen in their youth more of war than most professionals ever did. The knights might have called themselves professional soldiers, but if they did they were practically the only ones. The rank and file were generally yeomen or peasants who put aside their rural occupations for a short period to accompany their land-lord to the war. The lord kept a few men-at-arms, a small bodyguard of his own perhaps, and these were fully exercised in weapons, and probably uniformly caparisoned, but few knights could afford the upkeep of many such unproductive dependents.

War Companies such as Conan Doyle idealised in *"The White Company"* which could be hired by any wealthy sovereign to put backbone into his battalions appeared later.

As certain of the lower classes had to serve their landlords the Knights, so the Knights had to serve their feudal superiors; but for only forty days in any one year. A campaign lasting longer than that had to be sustained on some kind of rota system.

From all this one can see that the chance any leader had to adequately organise and drill his motley force was small. To obtain concerted action seems almost impossible. That they arrived on a battlefield prepared for action at all is surprising.

The enthusiasm of these warriors for a war, or for their cause, or for their leaders, may have risen high on special occasions: but when one considers the undeniable frequency with which they changed sides, broke faith, or turned their swords on each other, their comradeship so easily changed to hatred, one can no longer suppose that devotion to their cause was any solid foundation on which to raise a disciplined force. As for the rank and file in any muster of the period, the best of them, if not all, would be far more preoccupied with the prospects of getting home before harvest time. Many of their lives might depend upon the outcome of the imminent battle: but all their lives and their wives' and children's too, depended on the getting in of the harvest.

The idealism with which Simon managed to inspire his variegated host in the few days during their march to Lewes was lofty enough to give them the victory. But in less than a year so many had forsaken him or quarrelled with him that he had no power to prevent his own destruction at Evesham.

As there seem to have been as many barons on the King's side as on Simon's it is not clear why the army of the latter is always referred to as The Barons.

WHY AT LEWES?

It is always thought advisable, when about to fight a battle, to have an army stronger in numbers, or in weapons, or in courage, or in skill, or in intelligence than the enemy. In 1264 the King was hoping for help to arrive on the Sussex coast from his friends in France. If these reinforcements joined him before he encountered his enemy he was more likely to win the battle. For this reason he was keeping near the south coast, moving from east to west.

It was natural that de Montfort should wish to intercept the King before the royal army was augmented. He hurried southward from London and his route crossed the King's at Lewes.

Why the King was moving westward is not on record. He may have been expecting his French friends to land at Chichester, or at Shoreham, or even to have come up the Ouse to Lewes.

THE PARTICIPANTS

THE BARONS

Simon de Montfort was an eminent member of one of the most powerful noble families of France. He settled into English life at about the age of 30, having vast inheritances here. He married the King's sister. His obvious authority over both equals and superiors could have been derived only from within himself, as it was drawn from neither Emperor nor Pope. His commanding character inspired men to follow him to their own ruin or death. The renegades only betrayed him in success. He was over sixty at the time of Lewes, and had recently broken his leg. He fell at the Battle of Evesham a year later and was probably murdered on the battlefield when he could have been taken prisoner.

Among the notabilities on Simon's side were:—

Gilbert de Clare	a young lord newly knighted. He commanded the Centre of the Baron's army, in company with
John Fitz John	who was married to a daughter of a prominent Knight on the enemy side but remained faithful to Simon to the end.
William de Montchensey	served with him. This knight fought for King Edward later in the Welsh wars and was killed by the falling towers at the siege of Drossellan Castle.
Henry and Guy de Montfort	two sons of Simon, commanded his right wing.

Nicholas de Segrave commanded the left wing which was scattered by

Henry de Hastings	the first onslaught of the enemy. His request to lead the Londoners had been granted for his valuable past services. Years later he went to the Crusade with his present adversary Prince Edward. was another noted combatant. He prolonged the war even after Simon's death and was exempted from the pardons after the war, being condemned to seven years imprisonment. (Reduced to two by Edward).
John de Burgh	was grandson of the famous Hubert de Burgh who had governed the kingdom during the difficult minority of Henry III.
Roger Bigot	was Earl of Norfolk and, being Earl Marshal of England, had a special obligation of fidelity to the king he was now opposing.
Hugh le Despenver	may be noted as one who died with Simon at Evesham the next year.
Robert de Ros	was a great grandson of William the Lion of Scotland. He was charged with the custody of the prisoner Prince Edward after the battle.
John Gifford	appears from the records as outstandingly unpleasant among a society of greedy self-seekers. He was the only notable knight captured by the king's men on the field, although evidence shows him to have been one of the ablest soldiers present. He surrendered early in the day and was held in the castle. Yet even before this he had received the surrender of Sir Reginald Fitzpiers and Sir Alan de le Zouch, and the general suspicion regarding Gifford was augmented by the peculiar fact that both these knights were found free a few hours later. Fitzpiers fighting again, and Sir Alan disguised as a monk in the crowded priory. Later Gifford claimed payment of Sir Alan's ransom which Simon refused him owing to the dubious circumstances. It was this Gifford who won the first battle of the English long bow when he defeated the Welsh on the banks of the Wye in 1282. And it was he that sent Prince Llewellyn's head to the Tower of London with its crown of ivy.

THE ROYALISTS

Henry III This king, the son of King John, was now near 60 years of age and had been crowned for 48 years. His continued efforts to evade the consequences of his father's Magna Carta involved him in repeated disputes with the Barons, culminating in the Battles of Lewes and Evesham. He was a religious and highly cultured man, extravagantly supporting the arts. His deceits and perjuries appear excessive even among the contemporary nobility, but that may be only because his were recorded while theirs are lost in oblivion.

Richard of Almaine Richard was King Henry's brother. His native title was Duke of Cornwall. In the questionable and complicated European power-politics of the time he had emerged with the title and authority of "King of the Romans, Always August."

Prince Edward Edward was the son of Henry III, 25 years old at the time of the Battle. He was high-spirited and experienced in bearing arms but he had not seen a full scale battle, as such events were rare. He grew up at a time when the immortal legends of the Knights of the Round Table were first making their impact on literature as retailed by the troubadours in castles and palaces: And it is clear that his "strategy" at Lewes was derived more from their cloud-cuckoo-land than from the military text books on Caesar and Alexander. But he learned his lesson at Lewes and never repeated his error, for he was the man known later as The Hammer of the Scots. Ascending the throne on the death of Henry ten years after the Battle of Lewes he sensibly planned a pacific unification of the varied states of the British Isles. When his peaceful scheme was wrecked by accidents and ambitions which kings have not the power to avert, he resorted to war and in two campaigns, quite uninfluenced by tales of Sir Launcelot and Sir Galahad, rapidly conquered Wales and Scotland. Then the thickness of the veneer of Chivalry could be recognised by all who saw the severed heads of both Llewellyn of Wales and Wallace of Scotland side by side on the Tower of London at the conclusion of those wars: As they could also perceive the romance of transporting the Stone of Destiny from Scotland to Westminster and presenting the Welsh with a new Prince, born in Wales and unable to speak a word of English — his own infant son. But this all lay in the far future.

John de Warrenne   This de Warrenne, the Seventh Lord of Lewes, to whom the Castle was home, was the husband of King Henry's half-sister Alice. His story is the most extraordinary of any of his race. He was about thirty in 1264, and he and Prince Edward are the only warriors who took the field at Lewes and lived to be inscribed on the Roll of Caerlaverock during the conquest of Scotland in 1301. He held the Earldom for 53 years. What we know of his record is not endearing. When the war was over he challenged Henry de Lacy to a pitched battle over some property. The King forced them to settle by law, and as de Lacy won the case de Warrenne attacked the Chief Justice in Westminster Hall, wounded him and his son and fled to his stronghold at Reigate. He was brought to submission by Prince Edward, his late comrade on the field of Lewes, and the Archbishop of York, and heavily fined. Also he had to go on foot through the streets from The Temple to Westminster Abbey with 50 retainers and swear that he had acted in a sudden passion and not from malice. When Edward I, tidying up the kingdom after the wars in 1276, issued his celebrated Writs of Quo Warranto, demanding to know of the great landowners by what warrant they held their manors and estates, and to examine their title deeds, this was the man who took down from the wall of the hall in Lewes Castle the antique sword wielded by his ancestor at Hastings and flourished it at them meaningly: *"This is my warrant.* King William did not conquer this realm all by himself." In 1286 his only son was killed in a tournament at Croydon. His daughter married John Baliol, who became

King of Scotland. Baliol's father fought at Lewes with de Warrenne. In the Scots War de Warrenne was made Governor of the Scottish Conquests for his victorious services until he was chased from the field of Stirling by Wallace just as he was from Lewes in his youth. He was sixty-four at Stirling. He died four years later, and the church sanctioned a remission of 3,000 days in purgatory to those who prayed for his soul. He was buried in Lewes Priory, and as his bones seem not to have been recognised among those thrown out to let the railway cut through, he probably still lies under the earth covering those ruins. His tomb would be recognised by the inscription which it is said to bear in antique language:
> Thou that do tread this quiet way
> Forget not for the dead to pray.
> The bones that in this tomb are laid
> In life's fair bloom were once arrayed.
> Like them shall thine in Time consume
> And others trample on thy tomb,
> John Earl of Warrennes buried here.
> May mercy his good spirit cheer.
> For his repose whoever prays
> Wins forgiveness for three thousand days.

John Baliol a prominent lord in Scotland, was married to Earl Warrenne's daughter. He lost his Scottish lands when convicted of treason. In 1263 he had established scholarships at Oxford, and it was his wife that founded the renowned Baliol College. In 1292 his son became King of Scotland.

John Comyn who fought at Lewes, was grandfather of the Red Comyn murdered by Bruce at a peace conference fifty years later.

Robert Bruce Earl of Carrick, was grandfather of the future Robert Bruce, victor of Bannockburn and hero of Scottish history.

ARMS AND ARMOUR

The battle was fought many years before gunpowder was introduced. There were no guns, bullets or bombs.

The fighting was done with lances, or spears, swords, axes, maces and bows and arrows.

The sword was the distinctive mark of the knight or horseman, but he carried a lance for the charge. He might use an axe or a mace instead. The foot soldier carried a spear, about half as long as the horseman's lance, or a bow with arrows, and possibly a sword.

It is clear that man's power to do others harm had not advanced very far. Against an unclad person it is likely that, with a little unfriendly practice, a single well aimed and powerful blow with any of these weapons could be fatal, though even under such favourable conditions it is more probable that several blows would be required. But the sort of warriors that gathered for battle at Lewes had no intention of taking the field unclad.

MAIL

All who could afford to do so wore defensive armour: So there were some who looked like iron men, being completely cased in mail consisting of chain links rivetted closely together, reinforced in some cases with plates of steel. These men, practically all knights, were almost indestructible, as the sharp edges and points used against them would not penetrate their mail. Charged at full tilt with lance in rest, it is true, the links could fly asunder and let death into the interior. Or a foeman might deal a mighty blow with a battleaxe or mace and shatter the chainlinks and whatever was underneath. How often such lucky chances occured in battle can only be surmised. Dangerous bruises were inflicted even when the weapon failed to penetrate.

The less wealthy trooper protected as much of his person as he could with tough leather. If hand-to-hand fighting lasted more than five minutes, the number of weapons retaining a sharp cutting edge was small. Tough leather for helmets or shoulder plates would be adequate to foil most of the blows that did happen to make contact.

Even the poorest rankers padded out their costumes with some more or less protective matter.

In addition to this they all carried the largest shields they could conveniently handle. The horseman had an advantage as he could bear a long shield reaching from shoulder to ankle. The foot soldier needed something handier and lighter, so his was smaller. Shields were made of wood reinforced with iron or leather.

The horsemen wore "pot helms," called so because they were often really shaped like inverted cooking pots without the handles but with eye-slits.

Lastly, the sword itself was an effective defensive tool, used to parry or divert the opponents' strokes.

Effective homicide under such circumstances was difficult and commendably rare compared with the slaughter of more modern times.

The sword, less than a yard long, made of steel, with two cutting edges and a cross-piece hilt was the favourite weapon. It could be used for both cutting with the edge and thrusting with the point, on foot or mounted.

Lances and spears were tough wooden poles with leaf-shaped steel spikes fitted on their ends. The throwing spear of the Romans seems to have disappeared The horseman tucked his lance under his arm to charge; or raised it in his hand to stab in the mêlée or in chase of a dodging fugitive. The footman levelled his spear to run at his enemy or, close in his ranks, presented his point for the attacking horsemen to hurl themselves on if they, or their horses, dared.

Although archery had played so decisive a role at the Battle of Hastings (1066) when an arrow hit the King in the head, and at Stamford Bridge (1066) where the King of Norway was pierced in the throat, it seems to have been held in low esteem. The all-conquering long-bow of the next century was not yet developed. Actually it was John Gifford, who fought at Lewes, who has the distinction of being the first known commander to employ a company of long bowmen in war a few years afterwards. Bows were small and inaccurate and arrows could be dodged or caught harmlessly on shields, as, unlike bullets, they could be seen coming through the air. They were rather dangerous to horsemen as horses were often unarmoured. Struck by arrows horses could become unmanageable; and if his horse was brought down the knight fell and had to fight on foot if he could fight at all.

The deadliest weapon of the days was the crossbow which usually consisted of a powerful bent steel spring with a stock. The "bolts" or short arrows from the crossbow were propelled with violence, and were the only missiles capable of piercing knightly coats of mail. But it is a peculiarity of the period that the knights at Lewes appear to have had a noticeable reluctance to hurt each other much and it is conceivable that on both sides the word may have been given to leave crossbows out of it. Actually the Pope, whose word was sometimes attended to all over Christendom, had requested Christian princes not to use the crossbow as it was too barbarous except for hunting animals and heathens. Both Henry III and Simon were very religious men and the brevity of the known Lewes casualty lists may be due to the Holy Father's humane pronouncement. (It was, however, a crossbow bolt that struck down Henry's uncle, Richard Lionheart at an earlier date, and crossbowmen were shooting without restraint in the following reign).

The defect of this weapon was its slow rate of shooting and it was because of this that the English later in the 100 Years War took to the longbow, which had a rate of delivery six times greater.

The war arrows of both cross and long bows were cruelly barbed, like the hooks fishermen use. Hunting arrows were not barbed as a rule, as they might easily be drawn from an animal and used often again. The war arrow was barbed so that the wounded but tough recipient could not pull it out and continue to dispute the day. The range of the bow of the period is not known and its use in the Battle of Lewes is mentioned only in the shooting from the Castle walls and at the Priory in the evening, and not on the field of combat.

The mace, a short iron or wooden shaft loaded with a metal head, possibly spiked, was sometimes used by a combatant who saw only the ruin of a sword's edge on steel coats.

The battleaxe too could do more damage than a sword in the hand of a knight strong enough to fight with it. It had a much thinner blade than the head of a woodman's axe.

SHIELDS

A word has been said about shields.

By 1264 the warrior's shield had become something more than a protection. The practice of Heraldry was now ubiquitous. Each noble took for his family a distinctive device which was called his Armorial Bearings or Coat of Arms. Had it happened today it would have been "Credit Bearings" or "Coat of Commerce", as fame and power are associated now with money. Then, all nobility was identified with military service and arms. One of the prime reasons for choosing a coat of arms was to have a design that could be displayed on a banner or a shield as a kind of advertisement and identification mark in warfaring.

To avoid the adoption of the same "bearings" by several families, which would be confusing, official Heralds had been appointed by a

Royal College of Arms to approve and administer the designs. It became a common practice throughout Christendom, and it was part of a gentleman's education to know many of these, native and foreign. Even today everybody is familiar with the Armorial Bearings of the Kings of England: and the various Spread-eagles, Fleurs de Lys, Crosses, Chequers, beasts, birds, fishes, chimaeras, monsters, chevrons, bars and quarterings of Heraldry decorate the signboards of half the inns of Britain even now.

The "Blazoning" of these "arms" would have soon become as inartistically deplorable as the advertisement hoardings of the 20th Century, but for a simple rule enforced by authority from the beginning. No coloured object could be shown placed on another colour. Thus (for instance) no red lion ever appeared on a blue shield: No purple cross was allowed upon a field of green' A colour must go on a metal or a "fur", and vice versa. A man was not allowed a golden crown on a silver shield. Gold or silver must go on a colour or fur.*

By this simple aesthetic rule the panoply of Heraldry was saved from the fate of things in diverse hands like many of the flower beds in public parks which are riots of fine colours intermingled and cheapened by lack of either taste or discrimination. Thus a host of heraldic flags and shields had a dignified splendour. That this splendour cast its glow over the dubious human activity known as war was unfortunate. It became customary for every man of noble birth to have his coat of arms emblazoned on his shield. This was the more desirable as the improvements in armour resulted in the face of the warrior being masked in steel. He could now be recognised by the device upon his shield.

It was through the borrowing of a shield that the heroic brothers Balin and Bolan in the most tragical of the Legends of King Arthur, so popular at that date, came to their melancholy end:— "Alas Balin my brother, I have slain thee and thou me, wherefore the wide world shall speak of us both. . ."

It seems that Lewes field was the first battle in England to be fought since the heralds had systematised the blazonings. The earliest known Roll of Arms, containing the details of 218 Coats of Arms had been drawn up at the knighting of Prince Edward, ten years before he fought at Lewes.

So when the Barons came over the summit of the Downs and the Royalists trotted up to meet them on this day of battle, they saw

---

* *Fur, i.e. ermine, vair, or sable, was represented by ingenious stereotyped patterning.*

the famous high armorial bearings as they would be seen on no battlefield ever again, complete and original — not as they appeared later, quartered and requartered and slashed by dexter and sinister bars, as family intermingled with family.

It is a melancholy thought that the blue and gold chequers of the present arms of Lewes were to be seen fleeing from the field of fame on that memorable day, shining on the shield-arm of the mighty Lord of Lewes Castle as he ran for the escape bridge and disappeared over the Caburn.

THE ACTION

On the morning of the 24th May 1264, King Henry's forces were lodged in and around Lewes. Here de Warrenne was in his own home castle, and many chiefs including Prince Edward lodged here with him while the two brother kings Henry and Richard accepted the comforts of the great Priory on the marsh's edge below.

The rest of the troops were billeted in the Friary near the town bridge, in St. Nicholas's Hospital, and in the dwellings of Southover, Cliffe, Westout, and the town itself.

Perhaps it was unknightly to send out scouts to ascertain the strength of the enemy, where he was, and what he was doing. Their gallant attitude may have been one of contempt, believing that they could defeat him anywhere, at any time, under any circumstances. It is only recorded that a sentinel was stationed on the summit of the Downs overlooking the Weald.

The army of Simon de Montfort's barons had spent the night in and around the village of Fletching, about eight miles north of Lewes. They are said to have spent some time sewing white crosses on suitable aspects of their persons in order to distinguish friend from foe in the imminent chaos of battle. How they would have fared if by happy chance the enemy had done the same was not put to the test. A practicable track led through the woods and commons southwards to the gap in the Downs at Lewes.

There can be no doubt that Simon was well informed of the disposition of the King's forces. Before the 24th he had sent a deputation including the Bishops of London and Worcester to assure the King that they intended no harm to him and to inform him of their undying fidelity which caused them to strive to rescue him from the undesirable companionship of those "many about him".

The field now containing the derelict ruins of the old Priory had been the scene of a memorable spectacle on the previous day. It was thronged with the highly coloured costumes and arms and armour of the highest families of the age of chivalry all seen against a decorative background of graven walls and stained glass windows. Two kings and two princes were there. John Comyn was there, with Robert Bruce and John Baliol who were to make Scottish history together. Down Keere Street from the Castle came Prince Edward, Prince Henry and John de Warrenne to join the discussion. Around them in the chapter house crowded Lords, Earls, Knights, Squires and Bishops. Their massive crested helms blocked the window cills. Their multi-coloured shields hung from every vantage on the walls. Spears and lances with emblazoned pennons and banners were stacked everywhere. And as if to throw up the more effectively the magnificence of the scene, the Black Monks themselves, protesting but still serving, moved to and fro striving to minimise the damage likely to ensue from the entertainment of these boisterous guests.

The younger nobles grew more boisterous as, King Henry having dictated his defiant reply to Simon's dutiful letter, Prince Edward called upon his fellows for suggestions for an answer from those "many about him" that were insulted by Simon. These young warriors were not reluctant to furnish him with scurrilous and saucy repartee; and the ribald wit and horseplay and laughter with which they embelished the reply had to be reduced by the sober scribe to a literary form more suitable to the history books of future ages.

The King's reply had been reasoning and reproachful in tone, though ending with: "wherefore, of your favour and assurance we set little store, but you, as our enemies, we utterly defy".

The younger men's reply emerged as follows:—

"Richard, by the grace of God, King of the Romans, Always Augustus, and Edward the noble first begotten son of the King of England (etc.) to Simon de Montfort and all their false fellows.

By the letters which you sent to the King, (etc.) we understand that we are defied by you — wherefore we will that you understand that we defy you as our mortal and public enemies, and whensoever we may come to revengement of the injuries that you to us have done we shall aquit it to the uttermost of our powers. Where you accuse us of neither good nor true counsel to our sovereign lord the King you therein say falsely and untruly. If that saying you will testify in the court of our sovereign lord we are ready to give you surety and safe-coming, that there we may prove our true and faithful innocence, and your false and traiterous lying.

Witnessed with the seals of Richard, King of the Romans and Sir Edward forenamed. Given at Lewes the XII day of May".*

The two bishops rode off through Offham and Chailey towards

Old Style Dating.

Fletching. Now, it might be supposed, the King's men, knowing that words were done with and only blows would decide matters, would prepare at all points for battle and despatch scouts in all directions to give timely warning of every possible hostile move. If they did they were served incompetently. For at some time early in the morning of the following day the sentinel on the Castle tower sounded the alarm informing anybody who might be interested that the enemy were in sight on the hill above Offham, little more than a mile away.

Perhaps Henry was incompetent: Perhaps he was misinformed: Or perhaps he merely disdained his foes completely. It would only have been rational to have had his forces in possession of this commanding hill unless he meant to retire inside the town walls. It is recorded, as usual, that Henry's look-out on the hill had fallen asleep.

Before dawn Simon de Montfort had his army on the move southward from Fletching. At many points in their route they could glimpse through the trees the gap in the Downs wherein Lewes lay. Two miles north of the town they had the choice of two courses before them. The main track or road skirted the foot of the hills and kept close to the river bank to reach the landport of the town, now, marked by the Elephant & Castle Inn. To be caught strung out along this narrow pass between the steep hillside and the riverside marshes would be disastrous. So Simon chose the second course and took the whole army up the northern slope of the Downs above Offham to look down upon the town, castle and priory from the vicinity of the later racecourse. There is a convenient and very ancient track up which they may have dragged any wheeled vehicles they had, but there was no reason why the army should not have spread out and climbed up on a broader front less vulnerable to sudden attack.

Reaching the summit, unimpeded and with no enemy to be seen, Simon must have inferred that the King meant to fight a defensive action from the security of the town walls; until he saw the war flags and pennons streaming out of the northern sally-port of the Castle and the two nearer gates of the town far below.

As soon as he observed this inexplicable movement he halted his forces and gave the order for battle array. He had arrived in a perfect position for a battle and needed only a short time to take full advantage of it, if indeed the warriors below were actually coming out to fight uphill in the open.

At first sound of the war trumpets from the castle towers Prince Edward and de Warrenne rushed to the embrasures and verified without delay that the enemy whom they had so cheerfully defied the day before were almost hammering on their gate. Even without binoculars, plainly on the skyline of the open Down, they could see moving companies of glittering cavalry and foot soldiers already deploying under the bright banners of their lords and beginning to take up positions in their assigned battle order. There seemed to be not too many of them in order yet; and it appeared to the unhesitant mind of Prince Edward that if he could only launch an attack at once, even with only a few of his champions, before the whole of Simon's army completed their array on the summit, he might still counter their advantage with one dashing and courageous stroke. He despatched his couriers to get the two kings on the move from the Priory at once and issued a string of instructions or orders while his squires rapidly laced on his mail, clamped his grim helmet into place and held his warhorse for mounting. With everyone near enough to hear him he emerged from the castle and led his warriors in an all-out assault up the hill. Whether they came out through the sally-port over on the Paddock side or from the Landport gate or the West gate is not recorded. Anyway, they must have gone up near the Victoria Hospital and over the ground now covered by the Neville Estate.

From the town, from the priory, and from all their scattered billets streamed the rest of the Royalist troops, hastily arming and grouping under the ensigns of their feudal lords, and making for the Downs in more or less orderly companies. The two Kings, fully armoured, rode with them.

So, in a manner of no other battle on record, these two inexperienced armies drew near to the shock.

At the top of Offham Hill the first baronial troops to arrive in position were the Londoners under Seagrave. Few of them could have had useful military experience, as there had been no sizable battle in England for 50 years. They were halting to wait for the bulk of their army to take station with them before a mass advance down the hill when the reckless chivalry of Prince Edward appeared coming up against them. Trumpets blew, couriers galloped, commanders shouted, and companies of the men with white crosses panted up from the north and wheeled into line, while the enemy horsemen coming up from the south began to gallop. Edward saw at last the actual device on the banner of Seagrave: he saw the flag of the London contingent: and he shouted approval within the hollow of his helmet, for no enemy in the world could have been more welcome to him. He gave the order and began to gallop.

The steepest part of the hill was already passed and the ground levelling out. There were three or four hundred mounted men with the Prince. They had ridden over a mile, uphill all the way. Now they lowered their long lances, just as in their tournaments and tilt yards, couched them under their arms, leaned forward in their saddles and charged in a mass against the London ranks.

The Londoners presented a formidable appearance, a wall of men bristling with spears which now at a trumpet call came down to receive the charge. Had they been able to protect themselves with a shower of effective missiles they could have injured so many horses that the attack would have been broken up and thrown into confusion. But there is no mention in the tale of either arrows or slingbolts. The London array looked more formidable than it was. Before the armoured Barons could get to their aid the Londoners were struck by the band of Edward's knights and their ranks burst asunder. They were scattered in the first shock, and in the dismay of finding themselves, half armed, at the momentary mercy of iron men mounted on unusually large horses of war, their courage failed and they ran for their lives. It is inferable that the main army of the Barons was still struggling up the northern slope of the hill, or their mounted warriors would have gladly galloped across to join issue with Edward. As it was he was left free to take his revenge on the luckless Cockneys. As they fled like rabbits his knights dropped their lances and drew their long straight two-edged swords to cut and slash at all they could overtake. They vanished over the brow of the hill towards Offham, leaving the Barons' army still massing itself for action up on their left. They chased their victims clear off the field, unable in their enthusiasm to restrain themselves. It is possible they supposed that in one deed of derring-do they had as good as already won the battle.

A strange incident occurred as the London battalion broke and fled. Among the other paraphernalia their slower followers had hauled up behind them was an extraordinary vehicle, a kind of iron cage on wheels, a mobile prison. Although it displayed the red shield with the silver lion of Simon de Montfort himself, it actually contained three leading London citizens who, having sided too openly with the King, were now the Barons' prisoners or hostages. It is difficult to believe this circumstance was unknown to Edward, or that he had failed to give instructions about it. But some at least of his riders had not been informed. Coming upon it in their exultant progress they must have taken the unfortunate occupants to be city fathers favourable to Simon's cause, for they galloped up to it, dispersing the lackeys, guards, or attendants, and with their weapons attacked their own friends in their aery cell and slew them before continuing the chase.

This pursuit of the fugitives, having had so great an influence on the result of the battle, exercises the chroniclers considerably. Cavalry charges are a thing of the past, but it is known that the great difficulty in such actions was to keep the horsemen together or to reassemble them in time to be useful again whether they had been successful or not. Even in the regular armies of a later date it was a protracted matter. In this case it is stated that the Prince's knights went downhill slaying their victims right down to the River Ouse where many were drowned trying to escape across the water near Hamsey. Others say the pursuit continued for four miles, presumably in the direction of Barcombe. One, more foolish still, actually mentions that they halted only at Croydon forty miles away.

At least it seems true that Edward was so taken up with the pursuit that he returned towards the battlefield only when it was too late to be of use. Worse still, he had not effected the purpose of his blitz-like stroke. But this may have been because the Kings were too slow getting up the hill. For in spite of Edward's rapid action, the Barons succeeded in advancing over the top of the hill and commencing the array of their main battle order, while the shouting and clashing of the first onset died away over the hill towards the north-east, the river and the Weald.

From this moment it should be possible to give a clear and reasonable account of the contest. The stories of other battles are comprehensible, but the tale of Lewes is ill-reported, so that much has to be deduced from the fragments. Let it be supposed that Edward's reckless ride up the hill occupied a quarter of an hour, as even he could hardly have been so foolish as to have galloped all the way and arrived with gasping horses for the outright charge at the top. But even an hour would be short measure for the King's army to assemble from town and priory and suburbs, to arm and form and set off uphill towards where the Barons were indicated.

Some had to assemble in the High Street and the old market place, others in Southover outside the Priory, more still in Antioch Street and the adjacent field known as the Hide, and many small companies fell in wherever they happened to be when the alarm sounded. Then, as 'gallopers' dashed from place to place with directions and commands, all began to converge towards the head of land marked then by St. Nicholas Hospital but later by the Junior School outside Lewes Prison. Those in the town marched rapidly out by the West Gate which straddled the High Street where the town clock is. Those from the Priory, joining with the numbers from Southover, crossed the almost dry bed of the Winterbourne in the neighbourhood of the Grange and St. Pancras Bridge and swarmed up over the present cemetery, contacting those from the town in the neighbourhood of St. Annes Church, and from then on covering the open unfenced country with a mass of several thousand horse and foot all facing and hurrying up towards the later racecourse grandstand. All began in confusion, and confusion ruled throughout the day.

For it was hardly to be expected that a motley and ill-disciplined collection such as this would move like clockwork or act in perfect unison even under favourable and prepared conditions. Some welldrilled companies were advancing up the slopes in compact order and with some show of military precision; others were aligning themselves as their commanders saw fit for the assault, while others were still only emerging from the West Gate; and lack of co-ordination strewed the landscape with picturesque battalions and companies of knights, men-at-arms, horse and foot, multicoloured and glittering with metal, streaming with one object to the field of battle, to come in sight at last of the enemy on the crest.

Simon, riding horseback in some discomfort with his injured leg, had gained the summit in time to see the charge of Prince Edward vanishing away on his left, and he dismissed it as a mere opening skirmish. He hastened the rest of his forces into position, extending them across the high, almost level ground between the Ouse valley on the one side and Houndean Valley on the other; that is to say from near the Grandstand on his right to the vicinity of the Offham Chalk Pit on his left. The advancing legions of the two kings were now visible coming up against them, and the accounts of what happened next imply that both armies were equally inefficient. The Barons at the top had not succeeded in completing their positioning, and the more eager Kings' men were not waiting for their slower contingents to form up with them before committing themselves.

If there was any plan at Lewes it can be neither discerned nor detected. No line of entrenchment, no remnant of stakes, no contemporaneous memorial, no hedge, no horse lines, give any evidence. The one army that could have used the adjacent massive defence works of Lewes that de Warrenne had built ready for war, and which would have ensured them the victory, marched out from their protection to be defeated in the open.

Here battle was joined before either Simon had got his forces adequately placed, or the Kings and Princes had concerted their action. Prince Edward had set a bad example and in much the same way each feudal lord led his battalion up the hill and rushed against the most convenient adversary.

Men-at-arms coming foot-slogging up saw bands of cavalry being chased down. They would present spears and plunge in to check the pursuers, presently to come up against another wall of footmen like themselves but not yet disordered by motion. They in turn would be thrown back, and knights on high horses would break in among them striking at their heads with long straight swords, axes or maces. Companies under wily leaders would try clever outflanking moves only to find themselves struggling in disorder up steeper inclines among bushes and furze. There seems to have been no great shock of battle as the two main armies met, but from the beginning the entire combat has the character of a vast incoherent skirmish in which the clarion calls went unheeded and the war horns sounded their directions in vain.

It was a unique sight for the ladies and sightseers gathered on the turrets of the Castle. The whole tilted landscape between the Grandstand and the Prison was alive with fighting figures and moving bodies of troops and the scene was all in view from where they stood.

For the armoured knights it was as much fun as a boar hunt or tournament. They were protected doubly, first by their expensive iron coats and next by the ingenious system of ransoms which made it most thriftless to kill a knight on the battlefield if it were even remotely possible to take him prisoner and hold him to ransom. One of the very few ways in which a poor gentleman could acquire wealth was by receiving the surrender of a noble opponent brought down by horsefall, wound, or overwhelming numbers. It is understandable that, although a knight of coat armour would never surrender to common soldiers of no pedigree, the soldiers would not dare kill him intentionally for fear of their own chief's wrath at losing his ransom. No ransom was normally paid for the dead body of even the bluest-blooded aristocrat: though after Hastings Harold's mother offered it's weight in gold for the corpse of her son.

Add to this that most of the combatants were related to each other in some degree — even Simon was the King's brother-in-law — and the whole quarrel appears almost a family affair.

In the general mêlée the knights levelled their lances and charged as they had a mind, singly or in companies, perhaps meeting a rattle of sling bolts or arrows on their shields every now and again from the lower classes who scuttled away behind clumps of furze when the ironclad champions spurred towards them. Now and again knights charged knights, armour clanged, French as well as English voices yelled together, warriors rolled on the turf, horses galloped riderless, hooves drummed the trembling earth with that thrilling and threatening noise now heard only on racecourses, and here and there a small disciplined troop trained by a veteran of the Crusades stood like an island in a swirling sea of weapons, banners, plumes and crests. And, of course, the inevitable mediaeval cry of "Traitor" rang out as from the eye slits in his helmet one fighter recognised an old friend now under a strange device upon the opposite side.

Then it could be seen that the whole panorama was slowly rolling downwards and the hilltop was left empty except for a sprinkling of limping figures and prostrate forms and the black shapes of monks moving in from the sidelines to carry out, even here, their ordained duties. Simon and the Barons were gradually forcing the Kings and the Princes down again towards the town. At first the movement was doubtful, the ground disputed yard by yard. But few stood to the death. Tough groups standing resistant to begin with, found themselves suddenly alone, attacked on three sides at once, and retreated slowly downwards in fair order. Between these the Barons, making good use of the advantageous slope they had enjoyed from the first, let loose their horse and foot all in one resistless advance. This was where Prince Edward's battalion might have changed history, but he was away out of sight. The whole army of the two kings began to dissolve or break up. Everywhere men were running, galloping, striking, shouting, yielding or manoeuvring like ants in all directions, but the whole battle was rolling down towards St. Anne's Church.

(One wonders if the unknown lady, walled up alive voluntarily in the side of that church and known to be there in 1253, caught glimpses of it all through any tiny window on the living world she allowed herself on that historic day.)

It was near there that a major combat developed round a particularly interesting banner that still waved over a defiant company of glittering chivalry. Richard, King of the Romans, had been caught in a rushing clash of colliding horsemen, was thrown to the ground, and found himself in great danger of capture by common men-at-arms whether he yielded formally or refused. From this intolerable disgrace he was saved by the few of his own champions near enough to have seen his fall, who now dismounted for his sake and ranged themselves with him. Back to back they stood with him, and saw no help anywhere on the field. Immediately around them were only men marked with white crosses, and as their eager shouts arose, all turned towards the grim-looking group of nobles and rapidly closed in on them. Cut off from further retreat, hemmed in on all sides, the humiliation of surrendering to common men of vulgar blood stared them in the face. But there was a windmill close beside them. To the desperate King it presented a refuge from the worst disaster. With his steel clad companions he cleft his way through the encircling mob and reaching the foot of the mill, retreated with them ponderously up the steps in a compact body with their faces to the foe. They got inside, battered and bruised but still on their feet, and barricaded the door to an irreverent chorus of rude catcalls.

It is instructive to consider from this incident how the concepts of chivalry, noble blood, and the ransom system affected the warfare of the Middle Ages. If this had happened in the Dark Ages the mill would have been set afire by the assailants, and its occupants burnt alive. Had it been in the 20th Century a hand grenade or two would be pitched through the window and the occupants blown to bits. But the King of the Romans, alive, might be worth £50,000 in these early days of chivalry. His uncle Richard had had to pay £80,000 ransom to get out of Austria, in spite of Blondel's well-known musical performance.

So while a few clods of earth and chalky brickbats thumped against the door and plumped through the open apertures, the exalted defenders were constrained only to endure the sarcastic jeers of "Are you a King or a miller?" and the ironic "Come out of it you King of the Romans"; with a derisive shout in chorus: "Always August!" A solitary commander named John Bevis (recorded as Befs) detached from the rout, joined them: and upon a voice from the mill demanding to know who they were, Bevis proclaimed himself a vassal of the Earl of Gloucester. The besieged monarch thereupon offered to surrender vicariously to that Earl. Bevis accepted, and King Richard came out under safe conduct, gave up his valuable sword, and was escorted in disgrace from the field. John Bevis was knighted by his overlord the Earl as soon as possible to regularise the matter. Complaining to the Earl of Gloucester about his ignominious situation, Richard was recorded as protesting: "I am a foreign monarch and take no part in local skirmishes". To which the Duke only answered "You've taken part in this one, and your brother too. For all I care you are the Earl of Cornwall. You've talked your way out too often. It will not avail you now."

The mill in which this regal affair took place is supposed to have stood near where the Black Horse Inn now stands. Nothing supports this supposition but tradition. In the 19th Century there were at least 2 mills between the prison and the racecourse, one of which may have succeeded the mill of the battle. No doubt excavation could reveal the truth.

This incident caused no halt in the general rout of the King's army. Back the way they had come, across Western Road, over the cemetery ground, Rotten Row, and Grange Road, and across the Winterbourne towards the Priory they retreated, Henry their king in their midst. Others crowded into the town again where Simon's troops got in with them and continued fighting in the streets and 'twittens'. Some of the fugitives re-entered the Castle and from the walls held off the foremost pursuers with missiles before drawing up the bridge.

As for de Warrenne, he galloped with all his cronies of a like mind past the massive walls of his own great castle, down the Paddock, past the Land Port (Elephant & Castle) over the town bridge and away towards the east. With him fled two or three hundred mounted men, including Hugh Bigod, William de Valence and Guy de Lusignan. His object, no doubt, was to get out of the country by ship from Pevensey so as to retain freedom of action for future occasions. The only puzzle is, why more chiefs, including Prince Edward, failed to do likewise.

Now, while crowds of Simon's troops swarmed in the streets and round the castle walls, more still were driving King Henry, Bruce, Baliol, Comyn, Percy, Bardolph, Bohun, Tattershall, Someric, Bassett (reputed the "last to yield") and disorderly crowds of their henchmen down to the bottom of the valley on the south side outside the town until all who could took refuge inside the sheltering walls which surrounded the Priory like the walls of a widespread fortress (and a few of whose stones are still to be located in the fabric of the dwellings in the neighbourhood). Those who could not crowd through the gates in time either surrendered or fled along the track to Swanborough or up Juggs Lane to the open country. Those who, according to the chroniclers, were drowned, must have been unfortunates who, unaquainted with local geography, tried to escape along Ham Lane which is reputed to have led to a ford across the Ouse, but which, if the tide was in, only landed them in the wide and trackless marshes that encompassed the Priory and the town on all that side. The records say that many were drowned or suffocated in the mud, and this is feasible only in this vicinity, where men encompassed by danger on every side might be tempted to essay the crossing of a ford at a time when the tide rendered its waters much too deep and swift for horse or foot.

However, when the Great Gate of the Priory closed, the King and many men of quality were temporarily safe inside while the multitude of pursuers ranged east and west outside the wall spreading out till they surrounded it. The battle draws to an end with the King's forces scattered into four categories: One batch of knights and their closer retainers shut up in the Castle; The King with a similar company enclosed in the Priory; a greater number fleeing up the hills to east or west; and lastly Prince Edward's detachment returning from their northward chase.

The chief mystery of the day is in regard to how long Edward was away during the main conflict. If his pursuit of the Londoners lasted only an hour or so, the battle itself must have been of very short duration, as it was all over when he returned. On the other hand, if the battle lasted any length of time, what could he have been doing for such a period? There is no answer to this.

When he reappeared, all had been decided. Simon's troops were in the town making ready, as it seemed to the Prince, to besiege or assault the Castle on which friendly banners could still be seen. If he had truly lost count of time (none of them carried watches) it is possible that he had conceived the obvious plan of riding back from Offham unseen along the base of the hill near the Ouse, to turn in towards the battlefield across the Neville Estate ground and thus execute the sort of flank charge against Simon that is much approved in military affairs.

If he did, his feelings may be imagined when he arrived over the side of the hill to find nothing before him but the dead and wounded scattered prone upon the sward and the few black-gowned monks trying to ensure Salvation for as many of the souls of the dying as possible before they departed out of this world.

He rode past the north-western ramparts of the Castle, which are coincident with the town wall, where one can approach the Castle wall without entering the town. Somehow he learnt that his father had retired once more into the Priory, and as it is unlikely that any of the odd companies of the enemy he now met or passed on his way would have told him, he probably learned the whereabouts of the others by shouting up a few questions from the vicinity of the Paddock to the men on the castle battlements that positively towered up on that side. Then he rode round outside the town, past the West Gate and downhill to Southover where he entered the Priory to rejoin the defeated chiefs. How, is left to surmise.

This clearly means that whether the battle was understood to be over or not, at least the fighting had died down; and it must have been recognised that the Prince should be allowed to proceed unhindered by Simon's army scattered round Castle and Priory: Or perhaps, meeting with the overwhelming body of Simon's Barons outside the walls in Southover, he simply yielded his sword and so was allowed to pass in to his father. Some accounts speak of him fighting his way through.

In any case, while the situation was still confused with small parties prolonging hostilities, — by the marshes, over the bridge, up Juggs Lane and around the Castle, and while some elements of the Baron's followers were shooting flame-tipped arrows over the Priory walls to annoy the occupants as much as possible before all the 'sport' came to an end, the Prince got into the Priory to stand by his father in his distress, and to agree that surrender was their only course.

When Simon's herald, standing just about where The Red House in Southover High Street now stands, summoned them to open the Great Gate and accept the Barons' terms, they decided to admit their adversaries and accept their terms.

It was dark before news of this capitulation took effect. The Barons' men in the town and about the Castle Ditches still not knowing if this were only the beginning of a campaign, were setting about preparations for the siege of the Castle, occupying and reconnoitering all the dwellings facing the Castle walls and rearing pavises at the approaches to prevent possible sallies. Who commanded inside the citadel now is not recorded, but the Royalist occupants manned the walls and from the embrasures, harassed Simon's men with arrows. The Barbican was unbuilt then. The men in the houses and yards replied in kind, upon which the besieged followed the example of their enemies down at the Priory and fitting their missiles with flaming tow, attempted to drive the besiegers further off by shooting into the thatched roofs.

As darkness fell men who had taken temporary refuge in buildings in the town emerged to get clear of the consequences, and clashed with Simon's men in the streets. In the descending twilight mediaeval Lewes presented a chaotic spectacle with combatants clashing and trampling to and fro shouting and cursing while the townsfolk barred their doors wherever they could and looked to the protection of their property, as insurance was unknown. As the flaming arrows took effect on the combustible dwellings round the Ditch, the lurid light of burning roofs supplemented the glow from the fires in the Priory, giving the active figures in the streets a lively and colourful impression of that red-lit Hell in which they all believed. But it lasted no great while before heralds arrived proclaiming the truce, which took effect at once. Everyone set about dousing the fires and they succeeded in saving the town and Priory from destruction.

The Battle was officially at an end.

On the following day King Henry set his seal to the famous Mise of Lewes, dictated by the victorious Simon, leader of the Barons.

NOTES

STRATEGY?

There is a memorable remark made by an observer as he stared aghast at the consequences of a famous military blunder. He said, critically, but fairly enough: "It is magnificent, but it is not war." He was mistaken. War is a long tale of blunders in which victory goes in the end only to the side making the fewest; or smallest, blunders.

It is best to bear this in mind: otherwise one might be inclined to conclude that the Battle of Lewes was a collision of two armies of mental defectives.

Of course many facts affecting it must be missing, yet it is difficult to even imagine what facts could explain the conduct of the commanders.

There is nothing in the accounts to suggest that Simon's force was two or three times as numerous as Henry's, which it should have been if it was his intention to assault such a fortress as Lewes.

Nor is there anything to show that Henry's array was twice as strong as Simon's, as it would need to be before contemplating a long charge uphill against an enemy arrayed upon the top.

If each commander imagined he was so vastly superior to his adversary, his intelligence department must have been inefficient.

The King was at Lewes, a walled town having also a citadel whose massive ruins even now would present a formidable resistance to attack with anything less than an atom bomb. Inside this defence system, which he had had time to further strengthen and prepare, Henry could have defied the Barons and derided their efforts until their patience and rations alike gave out and their battalions melted away. He did not do it.

But Simon could hardly have known the King would not do it. So why did he hurry to Lewes to meet almost certain disaster?

And why did Henry throw away the advantage of his fortifications and take his army out from a position of maximum advantage to fight in a position of maximum disadvantage?

The popular idea that the Middle Ages — In Days Of Old When Knights Were Bold — were a period of everlasting fighting may be or may not be true, but at least it is a fact that nothing like a full scale battle had occurred in England for fifty years or more. It cannot be supposed that military organisation or skill was of a very high order. Some knights had seen war on the continent and some like Richard, King of the Romans, had been to the Crusades.

There is an explanation of the extraordinary conduct of this battle but it, in turn, is equally far-fetched.

It lies in the literature of the period. The troubadours had recently come upon a mass of ancient British legends centred in the heroic figure of King Arthur, and had brought these, much embellished and Romanticised into all the courts and castles of Christendom, so that this generation had matured in a world of song and story coloured all through by the valiant exploits of the Knights of the Round Table. Indeed it was this very Prince Edward who, later as King, inspected the bones of King Arthur, held by the monks, and reburied them in a rich tomb with great pomp and ceremony at Glastonbury. The foundations of Chivalry and Heraldry had just been laid, not on the rocks of Reason and Commonsense but on the insubstantial clouds of Fantasy. Through the literary forests of these fascinating legends wandered the mighty figures of Launcelot, and Persival, and Tristram. The Sword in the Stone, the Dolorous Stroke, the Lady of the Lake, the Last Tournament, the Great Battle in the West and even the Horn of Roland were familiar to them all. Knightly encounters and desperate combats were in every song. In none of them is a hint of generalship. They do not mention strategy.

So perhaps it amounts to this, that Lewes has the honourable distinction of being the only battle ever fought exclusively on the principles of knightly chivalry. The two kings fought as brothers in arms. The knights charged in full armour with lance and sword: Heraldic coats of arms were all displayed. Each commander proclaimed his defiance: Neither side feared the foe or recked the odds: Both advanced headlong to the combat as to a festival: Mercy was shown to the defeated: Prisoners were taken: Nobody was murdered in cold blood after the victory.

Yet there remains a certain paradox about Lewes, in that although it befel in the very heart of the Troubadour era among people imbued with the 'Romance' epics, it seems to have registered on the mentality of the time more as a business deal or commercial transaction.

The troubadours, who might have entertained noble audiences for years with songs and stories based on the exploits of their noble friends, passed it by unsung Minstrels who should have provided themselves with a whole repertoire of popular chansons and ballads remained mute. And poets who thrilled the ages with the Song of Roland and the Mabinogion only recorded in the "Song of Lewes" a kind of dreary political treatise.

The probable explanation is that they saw the deeds of their ancestors in the rosy light of far-off things, but they themselves — like all of us — were modern, up-to-date, unromantic and matter of fact. The towers of the Priory in which they signed the Mise were as new as our latest office block and the place to them was as down-to-earth as a filling station, though their god was not speed. Their dominant consideration of ransoms was a mere matter of business. The losses of the defeated were simple rents, lost by forfeiture of estates. The whole quarrel was about power, not chivalry; wealth, not honour.

KING HENRY'S PROWESS

The king was nearly sixty years old, yet one chronicler relates that he performed so valiantly in the field that he had two horses killed under him, was much beaten with swords and maces, and that he escaped with difficulty.

Consideration of the conditions then prevailing suggests that there were few things that Simon would have deplored more than injury to Henry. If he had believed that there was any likelihood of the king venturing among the combatants he would have issued strict instructions that he was on no account to be hurt. They were fighting to save the king from his companions, even against his wishes. Henry's prowess and hardihood were probably more in evidence on the scribe's parchment than on the field.

THE FIGHT AT LEWES BRIDGE

The mediaeval chronicler states that hundreds of the defeated troops rushed to cross the Town Bridge to escape and that many were forced off into the river and drowned while others leapt in their haste to a similar fate. More, he says, fled into the marshes where numbers were swallowed and suffocated in mud pits, and many knights who perished there were discovered after the battle still sitting on their horses in complete armour and with drawn swords in their lifeless hands.

Picturesque embellishments such as these must be critically assessed. We may be out of touch with the behaviour to be expected of horses nowadays, but it is permissible to wonder if we are to suppose that the knights sat on their dead horses until they died too, or that by coincidence horse and rider expired at the same instant, or that the rider died and his steed then followed suit: and that the unfortunate warrior was unable to put down his sword in order at least to die a little more at ease.

It is true that under the urge of fear men can behave in deplorable ways. If some of Henry's troops were running away from the stricken field and it seemed that their only escape route lay across the town bridge, they might have begun to jostle pretty close together at the approaches. Then some could have found themselves pushed off the wooden structure. Even if knights were protected by their ransoms, common soldiers might think a chance of a ducking, or worse, in the river, worth taking, and push their way on if closely threatened from behind. But whatever happened at the bridge, if anything, it could not have affected the issue.

CASUALTIES

The numbers engaged in the battle are unknown. Estimates range from ten to forty thousand. The chronicler puts on record his sentiments:

> Many faire ladie lese hir lord that day
> And many gode bodie slayne at Leaus lay.
> The nombre none wrote, for telle them mot no man

But He that alle wot and all thing ses and can.

"The number none wrote", is the truth. If one likes guessing there are some figures touching the matter in the Collected Papers of the learned N. Denholm Young. After years of research exhausting all records he was able to trace the names of 390 gentlemen known to have taken part in the war, and he concluded from his studies that at that time there were about 1,250 knights, including earls and barons, in England, and that of these about 500 were actually fighting knights.

As nothing in the story indicates any dreadful shock of trained regiments against disciplined battalions, casualties were probably few. The nature of the fight precludes heavy slaughter. The difficulty of killing resistant armed men bearing protective shields, who do not really want to be killed, with feeble weapons such as swords and spears, or with visible missiles, is quite considerable. In such a battle as this it is clear that men in danger of being badly knocked about could, as the field was unlimited and discipline dubious, simply retreat a little, dodge, duck, take cover, or even remember his family and run away. If, in addition, all the more aggressive types were cased in mail "of proof" from head to foot with only eye-slits to see through, death found no abundant harvest.

In fact, it is recorded that two knights were killed on the Barons' side, Ralph Horingunder and William le Bland who was Simon's standard bearer. The same record says twenty-three of the King's Knights were slain, but only two of their names are known; William dc Wilton and Fulk Fitzwarren.

In 1810 the old lane that ran from Lewes to Brighton was reconstructed for the coaches, involving new grading. Just in front of where the Prison gate now stands the navvies uncovered three large pits full of human bones. No archaeological society existed at that time and no reliable account of the discovery remains, but it is said that the relics were estimated to be those of about 1,500 men, and that it took some days to cart them away for reburial in consecrated ground. If they were the bones of men only, no one could doubt they were relics of the Battle, as the position accords well with the site. It would be natural for the monks and their assistants to make one main mass grave at the lower end of the field and bring most of the slain down to it, though it would have been more in keeping with their Christian customs to have put them, there and then, in a churchyard, and St. Annes was near enough.

If there is truth in this it indicates that there were sixty common soldiers slain for every one knight. Considering such statistics, it is salutary to remember what happened regarding numbers in the 20th century when the authorities had all the resources of modern methods, statisticians, journalists and reporters, intelligence services, and a trained Observer Corps, as well as men who did not have to count on their fingers. On one special Sunday in 1940 the Royal Air Force destroyed nearly sixty German aircraft in battle over southeast England. This was officially announced as 180. Five years later a correction was made. No corrections were made regarding the Lewes bones.

Other human remains have from time to time been turned up in the vicinity of the great Offham Chalk Quarry. This would occur if no battle had ever happened, as prehistoric burial places are scattered all over the area and the remains of our ancestors come to light on all the neighbouring hills.

No kind of military relic was ever recorded in association with any bones to clinch their connection with the battle. On the other hand there is no record in the town of the use of plague pits either during the Black Death, or the Great Plague.

THE MILL

The leading authority on the Barons War is Blaauw whose monumental "The Barons War" is a standard reference. It contains an elaborate account of the Battle of Lewes, and it is typical of every aspect of the story of the Battle that the following should occur on page 201: "No precise spot on the Downs now retains the tradition of this mill, though it was pointed out long after by the name of King Harry's Mill. As it is distinctly described by two contemporaries as a windmill "with sayles" it must have occupied the usual situation for such structures on the ridge of the hill," while on page 357 *of the same work,* he wrote: "Richard's defeat was so rapid that he made his escape to a water-mill at hand. This watermill was on the Winterbourne Stream, the remains of which were traceable about 80 years ago."

THE OLD MEMORIAL

In the year 1905 a monument was set up to commemorate the Battle. It stands on the edge of Plumpton Plain about four miles from Lewes, and can be taken to indicate the battle site only by ignoring both records and reason. Its position may have been chosen by the well-meaning erectors because of the proximity of an ancient sign cut in the turf on the chalk. This cutting is in the shape of a cross, but it is so overgrown that it is difficult to locate. It has been suggested that the Black Monks of Southover cut it out to mark the site when they had finished tidying up the battlefield, but it is too far from the town and more probably has nothing to do with the Battle.